Workshop Wisdom:

DOLLHOUSE CRAFTING TIPS

from Nutshell News

Illustrated by Jim Newman
Compiled by Kathleen Zimmer Raymond
Edited by Andrea L. Kraszewski

Cover photograph realistically portrays a miniature dollhouse workshop, courtesy of *Nutshell News* magazine.

Copyright © 1992
Greenberg Publishing Company, Inc.

Greenberg Books
A Division of Kalmbach Publishing Co.
21027 Crossroads Circle
Waukesha, WI 53187
(414) 796-8776

First Edition
Second Printing, 1992
Third Printing, 1996

Manufactured in the United States of America

Greenberg Publishing Company, Inc., publishes the world's largest selection of Lionel, American Flyer, LGB, Marx, Ives, and other toy train publications as well as a selection of books on model and prototype railroading, dollhouse building, and collectible toys. For a complete listing of current Greenberg publications, please call 1-800-533-6644 or write to Kalmbach Publishing Co., 21027 Crossroads Circle, Waukesha, Wisconsin 53187.

Greenberg Shows, Inc., sponsors *Greenberg's Great Train, Dollhouse and Toy Shows*, the world's largest of their kind. The shows feature extravagant operating train layouts and a display of magnificent dollhouses. The shows also present a huge marketplace of model and toy trains, for HO, N, and Z Scales; Lionel O and Standard Gauges; S, and 1 Gauges; plus layout accessories and railroadiana. They also offer a large selection of dollhouse miniatures and building materials, and collectible toys. Shows are scheduled along the East Coast each year from Massachusetts to Florida. For a list of our current shows, please call (410) 795-7447 or write to Greenberg Shows, Inc., 7566 Main Street, Sykesville, Maryland 21784 and request a show brochure.

Greenberg Auctions, a division of Greenberg Shows, Inc., offers nationally advertised auctions of toy trains and toys. Please contact our auction manager at (410) 795-7447 for further information.

Lionel® and American Flyer® are registered trademarks of Lionel Trains, Inc., Chesterfield, Michigan.

ISBN 0-89778-289-5
Library of Congress Cataloging-in-Publication Data

Workshop wisdom: dollhouse crafting tips from Nutshell News
    p.   cm.
  Rev. ed. of : Dollhouse crafting tips from Nutshell news. c1992.
  ISBN 0-89778-289-5

  1. Dollhouses. 2. Doll furniture. I. Nutshell news. II. Title : Dollhouse crafting tips from Nutshell news.
TT175.592'3—dc20   92-33747
                                             CIP

TABLE OF CONTENTS

INTRODUCTION

There are many fascinating aspects to miniatures. Indeed, that adjective — "fascinating" — seems to be the one most frequently applied to this growing hobby. The delight miniatures holds for its devotees undoubtedly has many origins, but none seem so compelling as that which comes from viewing the world in a scale of one inch to one foot. From this perspective, everything is unexpectedly different — literally. What was once one thing becomes another.

The art of turning wooden coffee stirrers into beautifully finished "hardwood" floors, discarded Christmas tree lights into wine bottles, plastic bubble packs into washing machines, or thimbles into lamp shades offers endless intrigue to those who pursue it. In fact, in the most harmless and pleasant of ways, contriving can become addictive. However, the reader should be forewarned: this book could lead you to petty theft (of coffee stirrers and cream containers, for instance). At the very least, it could bring on a severe case of compulsive recycling. But for those of you who are willing to take the risk, the rewards in terms of creative satisfaction are great.

Jim Newman, whose name appears as the illustrator of this book, would be the first to admit that its real authors are the readers of *Nutshell News* magazine. For over ten years, those readers have been sending Jim the tips he has used as the basis for "Workshop Wisdom," the popular column appearing in each monthly issue of the magazine. We gratefully thank our creative readers of *Nutshell News* for so generously sharing their ideas with fellow hobbyists. "Workshop Wisdom" is read and loved by one and all, from the most sophisticated collector to the finest miniatures artisan.

There is indeed much "wisdom" offered in these projects from past "Workshop Wisdom" columns. It is the wisdom of imagination, whimsy, and creativity — of turning the ordinary and insignificant into something unique and meaningful.

Enjoy!

Sybil Harp
Editor, *Nutshell News*

ABOUT THE ILLUSTRATOR

Jim Newman has lived in the "fast lane" — literally — all his life. As a native of Britain and the son of a Royal Air Force career man, Jim grew up around air bases during World War II. From childhood, he was immersed in flying and spent much of his time building model airplanes and painting pictures of aircraft and battleships.

At age sixteen, Jim was flying sailplanes and powered aircraft and became a Royal Air Force cadet. He also raced and built motorcycles and sports cars, incorporating these interests in the artwork he continued to pursue.

After twelve years in Her Majesty's service, Jim joined the aircraft industry as an illustrator and draftsperson doing artwork and drafting designs for missile equipment, minesweepers, cars, and the celebrated Concorde.

Since coming to the United States in 1970, Jim has worked in the hobby field as a designer, model maker, and graphic artist. He is presently a designer of model airplane and boat kits for Midwest Products Company. A widely acknowledged authority on aircraft of all types and vintage, Jim is known for his detailed, exploded-view drawings of airplanes. His drawing of the Laird Super Solution hangs in the Air and Space Museum of the Smithsonian Institution in Washington, D.C.

Jim's skill as a graphic artist and his enthusiasm for model hobbies have easily translated to the dollhouse miniatures field. For more than ten years, he has been a regular contributor to *Nutshell News* magazine with his series of readers' how-to tips and techniques known as "Workshop Wisdom." When he isn't contributing his talents to *Nutshell News* and other hobby magazines, he still enjoys flying both radio-controlled model airplanes and full-size aircraft.

*H*ere's a unique idea — a chandelier hanging inside a glass dome. Obtain a card of Velcro discs from the notions counter, and use a dab of tub seal to stick one half into the top of the dome. Attach the chandelier and wires to the mating disc and press into place, securing the wires inside the dome with transparent adhesive tape; or, do as the burglar alarm people do — attach the wires to the glass with a narrow strip of clear lacquer. For wire, our contributor uses Walther's extra fine, brown enamel-coated copper wire.

*T*his unique display piece was designed to fit a coffee table. It is made from matte board, using a large bowl as a template to cut the circles. Overall height is 8" and each quarter can be designed to your choice — a bakery, a hat shop, a flower shop, etc. Set on a Lazy Susan, it is an eye-catching conversation piece for visitors.

*T*his unbreakable domed cover for your dolls or terrarium gives double pleasure — you can drink the contents first! Fill the two liter bottle with water to the desired height then stand it on a level surface to mark around with a fine felt pen. Cut on the line with a sharp knife, then pull off the bottom. Mount your doll as shown, then invert the cut bottle over the bottom piece.

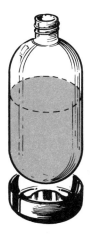

*O*btain a clear acrylic picture frame box from the craft or drugstore — an 11" x 14" is approximately $5. Build a room box from foam board or other suitable material, sized so that it will fit snugly into the frame as shown. No clips or other hardware should be necessary.

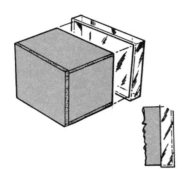

*N*atural willow-colored, "woven" wicker-looking, plastic needlepoint canvas provides a source of lattice for porches, summerhouses and screens. Just cut on the diagonal and use it where you will.

*T*his is a neat and unobtrusive method of securing a Plexiglas panel to the back of your dollhouse that remains quickly detachable. Screw brass cup hooks into the edge of the walls. To instantly remove the transparent panel, just twist the hooks to one side.

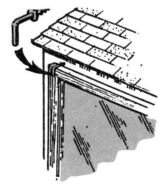

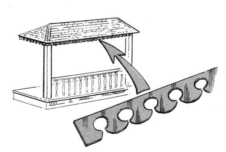

*H*ere's a nifty idea for ready-made trim for your gingerbread house. It is a strip of plastic, 1/4" wide and 13-1/4" long, used to retain Christmas tree lights in their display package. It can be cut and glued in place. Be sure to use only model enamels or acrylic paint on this plastic — it is most likely polystyrene and will soften under the action of some paints. Try out on a scrap piece first.

*F*inally, an economical method of purchasing siding that can be used with minimal waste — buy it by the roll! Obtain 1/2"-wide fiberboard tacking strip from an upholsterer. When painted with matte paint, it produces a very smooth exterior. Sketch shows how to mark the walls and glue the strips.

*S*imulate a pebble or cobblestone path. Select a thin sheet of white foam (Styrofoam R, for example), making sure the texture is appropriate for your application. Apply a coat of thinned acrylic paint. Wait a minute or so, then wipe off the excess paint, repeating the process as often as required. Trim to the shape required. Do not use cellulose-based glues or plastic model glues on this foam, it will dissolve immediately — white carpenter's glue works best. When painted dark brown this foam also resembles cork tile.

*H*ere's an intriguing material to use to simulate cement foundations or walkways. Available from most hardware stores, it is a sticky-backed, non-skid material for step ladders, etc. It comes in gray and other colors, and can be cut into irregular shapes to make crazy paving slabs in addition to regular sidewalks. At approximately 75¢ a running foot, it is quite inexpensive.

*E*asily create brickwork for small projects. Peel the top layer of paper from a piece of foam board. Score the brick pattern with an empty ballpoint pen or use the edge of a popsicle stick drawn along a straight edge. Seal the surface with artist's gesso tinted to resemble grout and, when dry, paint on the bricks using the appropriate color acrylic paints. You might find it easier to paint the foam brick red overall, then line in the grout with a small brush.

A pair of sharp end cutting pliers really speeds the trimming of cedar shingles. A trimmed sample is placed on top of the full shingle, which is quickly snipped to size. The plier jaws cover the full width of the shingle, so splintering is not a problem; and in any case, the trimmed end will be at the top, which is covered by the shingle above.

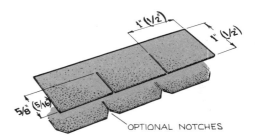

*I*f your shingles fall apart when trimmed at an angle, try this tip. Place the shingles face down on the sticky side of masking tape, then trim. After they have been cut, the shingles can immediately be glued in place on the roof. Once the glue has set, peel off the tape.

*L*aying shingles can be tedious. But if you sort them beforehand and lay them out pointing in the required direction, it makes the job so much more enjoyable. A quick trick is to set them on edge on the sticky side of masking tape. All the shingles are placed pointing in a direction which makes them convenient to pick and place.

*S*andpaper makes great shingles and can be obtained at any hardware or home improvement store. Select a color and texture which will complement your dollhouse, cut it into strips with slits as shown, and then glue to the roof with rubber cement. Rubber cement works best — ordinary white glue will cause the sandpaper to shrink and curl. The sketch shows two sets of dimensions (the dimensions in the brackets are 1/2"-scale).

*M*ake real, working shutter holdbacks by converting the Holdback No. 812 offered by Realife Miniatures. Obtain a piece of brass tube, 3/32"-diameter, from your hobby shop (K & S brand works well). Cut a suitable length sleeve from the tube. Drive a straight pin (instead of the nail supplied) through wall, then cut it off or bend it over.

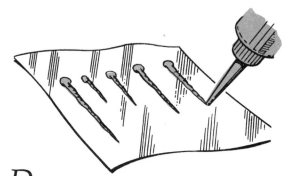

*D*ress your miniature house appropriately for the winter season with snow and icicles. Here's a simple way to create little icicles. Pipe a good quality white glue, like Elmer's brand, from a narrow glue bottle spout or a glue syringe. On a piece of plastic wrap, start with a dot of glue and pull it down into various lengths of tapering strands. While still wet, immediately sprinkle with fine white glitter and allow to dry for several hours before peeling away from the plastic. The icicles can then be glued to eaves, fences, window ledges and Christmas trees.

*I*n real homes, a windsock on the porch seems to be all the rage. Make your own with rainbow-colored hair ribbon, 1" wide x 2-1/2" long. Glue smaller colored ribbons along one edge, roll into a tube, then glue along one edge to keep the shape. Add a cord, then suspend it from the porch eave of your little house.

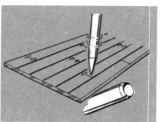

Create the illusion of pegs in an old-fashioned plank floor. Score across the floor at random with a sharp hobby knife, then twirl an empty mechanical pencil into the ends of the "planks." A piece of brass tube, sharpened with a fine file, also does an admirable job. Color contrast can be added by darkening the pegs with a felt tip pen, after which the boards can be varnished.

Planked wooden floors in your dollhouse are eye-catching, but can be expensive. For very few dollars and a visit to a restaurant supply store, it is possible to pick up a box of 1000 wooden coffee stirrers which make a convincing wood floor. After squaring off the ends, glue the stirrers down to the sub-floor and stain. Pierce tiny holes in the ends to simulate nails. Note the little 4" steel engineer's square in the illustration. An invaluable item on my bench, this handy precision tool (available in tool departments) is just what you need to square off the ends of those stirrers.

Here's an idea for a stenciled country floor for a miniature room. First, lay and sand the flooring. Lightly pencil on a grid as a guide. Then, using a rubber stamp with a stencil look and the appropriate color ink pad, stamp a regular pattern across the floor. Use a soft eraser to remove the pencil marks after the design is absolutely dry. Then apply a couple of coats of clear urethane varnish.

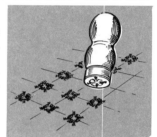

Plastic Slide Locks, used to bind the edges of reports sheets into folders and available from your office supply store, make inexpensive baseboards. Available in a multitude of colors at approximately 11¢ each, they can be cut down the center (see my dashed line) and painted to your preference using acrylic colors. Use a thick and tacky adhesive, like tub seal, to attach the baseboard to the wall. As for slitting the Slide Locks, try using a hobby blade glued to a suitable shim. Lay the Slide Lock on its side and run the blade along the spine.

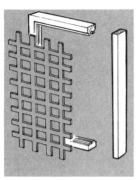

*S*ections cut from plastic strawberry containers, then spray painted, make unique room dividers which can be used to create interesting effects in your dollhouse or even a mini greenhouse.

*N*eed grillwork, mullions or divider screens for your dollhouse? Take a humble plastic berry basket and separate the individual sides as shown. The baskets come in all sorts of designs, so shop around. They can be cut with strong scissors, a sharp modeling knife or tin shears. Use plastic model enamel or acrylic paint, but handle carefully once the paint has dried because polyethylene does not really take paints.

*F*or ultimate realism in your dollhouse attic, glue strips of wood to the underside of the roof and above the ceiling of the second floor to simulate rafters and joists. Between these strips, glue strips of insulating paper (as found around the pipes of real houses), fuzzy side out. This insulating material resembles the insulating material found in real attics.

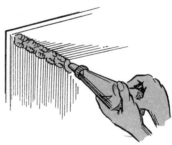

*M*any Victorian-era homes possessed fine plaster coving around the ceilings and even on the walls to frame superb hand-painted murals, some still seen in the fine old English city of Bath. Use cake decorating tips and pastry bags to pipe spackling compound into place in a design of your choice, then handle with care as you paint and gild the dry moldings. Clean up with soap and water before spackle sets!

*H*ere is a simple method for making Flokati rugs. Twist the cotton buds from Q-Tips brand cotton swabs into points with your finger and thumb. When you have accumulated sufficient buds, sew them to a piece of fabric until it is completely covered, starting at the edges and working in towards the center.

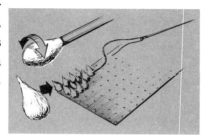

*T*rying to wallpaper around a mini staircase can be difficult. One solution is to make the staircase removable. Two little dowels at the bottom of each stringer secure the steps into the floor with the upper end of the staircase merely resting against the landing floor.

*F*luffy white felt can be turned into a beautiful bear rug when cut to the shape shown here. Add a head made from a cotton ball pulled to shape, then add eyes and a shiny black nose from suitable beads. Try cutting the pointed tips from white-painted toothpicks to simulate claws.

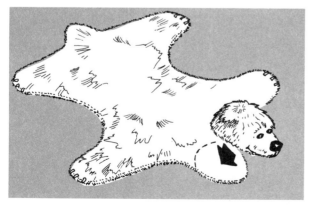

*H*aving trouble keeping your dollhouse door closed? Use a magnet! A small piece of tin (not brass, copper or aluminum which are non-magnetic) fixed to the back of the door and protruding upwards as shown, makes contact with a small piece of magnet cut from one of those magnetic note holders.

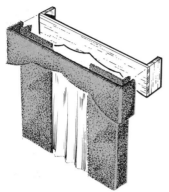

*M*ake a formal window treatment for a bay window. Build a valance from thin wood, then cut pieces of left-over mini carpet and glue them to the sections, wrapping them over the ends and sides. The side curtains are just vertical strips of carpet glued to the rear of the valance and allowed to hang. The finishing touch is a lace sheer glued across the opening.

*T*o put pleats or folds into mini curtains, pin the completed curtain to a piece of card, then spray it with hair spray — it will hold those folds forever. Remove the pins and hang the curtains when the spray has dried.

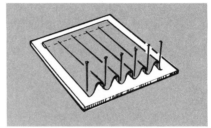

*T*he ruffle sometimes found around the bottom of old curtains or even a ruffled tie-back can be used to make simple gathered café-style curtains for dollhouses.

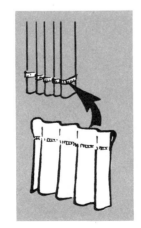

*T*his is an exceptionally simple method of hanging drapes which makes it very convenient to remove them for cleaning or rearranging. Use little Velcro buttons as shown in the illustration.

*R*ibbon-beaded lace, 3" long, makes a great material for little café curtains. Use a strip of tear-away backing as support while running a zig-zag stitch down the edge of the ribbon, then fold a "hem" around a thin dowel, securing it with a drop of glue. Add a small bead at each end of the dowel curtain rod before fixing it to each side of the window frame.

*S*ituate your dollhouse in any location you want. Give it a beautiful view across a river, see the World Trade Center, or a picturesque countryside. Simply tape a picture postcard across the back of the window aperture. You could also position a large poster a little way back from the house so that you would see the same view from each rear window.

*B*rass drapery rods are simply made by selecting a size of brass tubing with an inside diameter that will snugly fit a miniature brass door knob or drawer pull, which should then be carefully glued into the tube after the rings or drapes have been threaded on to it. Polish the brass tube and protect the shine with a thin application of a clear lacquer.

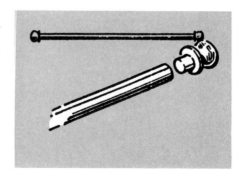

*T*urn discarded plastic 35mm film containers into great little tub seats. Use a sharp knife to cut as shown, then use contact glue to adhere suitable fabric covering. Cut a cylinder of sponge foam rubber, cover with material, and push the cushion down into the seat. (The lids can be used to make clocks, too.)

*W*hat a neat table top for a miniature contemporary café or ice cream store! Smucker's brand jellies and jams have lids that are printed with a delightful checker pattern and are without the usual manufacturer's name. Hot-glue a wooden door knob or something similar to the underside to complete the assembly. Of course, the really talented miniaturist can fashion "wrought iron" legs from thin brass strips.

*H*ere's a cute idea for an ice cream parlor set. All these pieces started life as Jet Dri dishwasher baskets, Smucker's jelly lids, fabric and fleece scraps. Trim the baskets to shape, cutting portions from other baskets for chair backs. Assemble as shown using dabs of hot glue. The chairs can be upholstered with scraps of sponge foam and fabric or fleece.

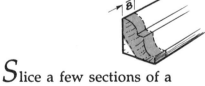

*S*lice a few sections of a piece of 1/2" x 1/2" crown cornice. When trimmed as shown, the slices make fine feet for piano stools, coffee tables, lamp stands and more.

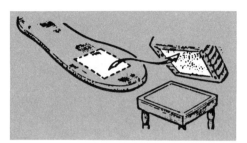

*L*atex foam sheet with self-adhesive backing, available from the drugstore under the brand name Dr. Scholl's, is just the right thickness and texture for upholstering chairs and sofas. No gluing is necessary — peel off the release sheet and it's ready to apply. It would also be practical to tuck the material under the cushion where it would be held by the adhesive, leaving enough "stickum" to attach it to the chair.

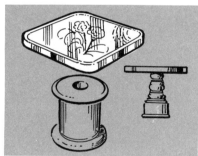

*K*eep an eye open for ceramic tile coasters — they make great café table tops. Use hot melt glue to attach them to lamp finials, drawer pulls or thread spools which can be decorated with decoupage. Mount them on discarded, cut-down chess pieces for a more traditional look.

*B*utcher block countertops or tables in miniature can be created by sawing 1/8"-thick strips off the end of a good quality piece of plywood, then gluing the strips side by side. When dry, sand thoroughly then varnish — the result is positively beautiful.

*C*reate attractive tables using wooden plaques. Found in most art and craft stores, they come in many attractive styles and usually cost less than $1. Stain, polish and attach suitable legs.

*E*asily create a veneer inlay for a table top. Find a color photo exactly the size required in a woodworking catalogue, and cut it out. Spray it with a couple of coats of clear Krylon sealer and decoupage it to the table top. You might even try flowing a thin coat of clear resin over it in place of decoupage — just like the real ones.

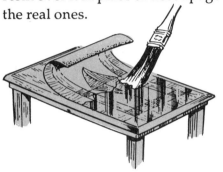

*F*or more realistic clock faces, cut clock faces from old clock catalogues. The glossy paper is much more life-like than the usual printed dial. With the glass in place, the effect is quite magical.

*I*n the center of some take-out pizzas is a small table-shaped plastic molding designed to prevent the box lid from collapsing onto the contents. Thoroughly cleansed and painted with a wood grain finish, using light and dark paints applied with a dry-brush technique, this makes a wonderful little table — and the price is right. Consider adding a table cloth, too.

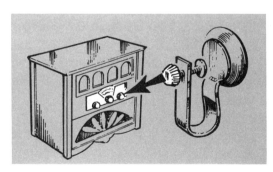

*S*imulating the appropriate style of knobs on a miniature 1920s radio is as close as your ears. Simply remove the knob and stem from screw-type earrings, paint to suit, drill holes, and then glue the stem and knob into front of radio.

*N*eed good, firm stuffing for a cylindrical bolster? Obtain a few of those tightly rolled cotton dressings or swabs that your dentist uses. Cover with appropriate fabric and glue a tiny button on the ends for a convincing look. You can even try using pairs of cylindrical foam earplugs, contact-glued end-to-end. They are inexpensively available from local sports shops or airport.

*S*witchplates, found in a variety at your local hardware store, make great decorative headboards. Various sizes of switchplates yield headboards for both double and single beds. Just cut across at a suitable height (see the sketch) — the effect is terrific. Imagine a crisp white and gold headboard!

*T*he cap of your typical flip-top shampoo bottle can easily be converted into a convincing garbage can or diaper pail. Cut out the top as shown, then glue in a circular plastic or thick card bottom. For a more interesting effect, the bottom should be just a little smaller than the diameter of the cap to give a distinct step in the side view.

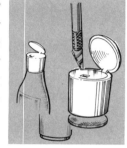

*T*his cute little rocking cradle is made from two walnut shells, cutting one in half to make the hood. Paint flat white inside then decorate by gluing in lace edging, small pillows, bows, and roses around the outside. Cut two wooden rockers and glue them to the bottom of the cradle.

*T*his neat infant seat is cut from the handle of a milk jug. Make slots with a No. 11 X-Acto blade, then glue narrow ribbon or flat elastic in place. Make a very thin pad from a wire twist tie and cover with a small print fabric.

A good adhesive or cement for assembling stone fireplaces is concrete patch as used in caulking guns. Just build up a wood form from 1/16" balsa or basswood, squeeze on some patch, then push the stones into it. The concrete patch which oozes between the stones should be smoothed or stroked with a simple tool made from a bent coat hanger wire.

*H*ere's a marvelous idea for a hooded fireplace. Cut a suitable plastic bottle as shown. Smooth the cut edge by sanding or pressing against a hot plate. The flue pipe can be extended to size with cardboard tube or, if required to go out through a wall, use a copper plumbing elbow. Painted matte black or metal, the effect is realistic. Look through home-decorating magazines for more examples.

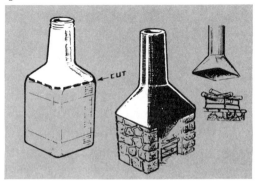

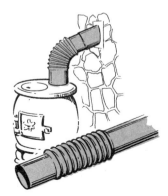

*S*ee that convincing corrugated stovepipe disappearing through the wall on that old potbellied stove? It's made from one of those bendable drinking straws so beloved by children. Trimmed to length, painted dull black and set in place, it couldn't work better.

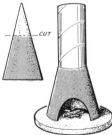

*T*his convincing fireplace is all Styrofoam, starting with a cone cut to the required height and hollowed out (as shown) before gluing to a foam hearth. The chimney is a toilet tissue card tube glued to the top, high enough to touch the ceiling of the room. The whole assembly is then coated with scale stucco and sprayed with a matte black paint. Do not use cellulose paints on foam — it will instantly dissolve. Use only water- or urethane-based paint or enamel suitable for plastic models. Testors is a good brand name and is readily available wherever plastic model kits are sold.

*B*ring the warm glow of a flickering fire to your dollhouse by mounting a photo of your own fireplace in the back of your mini fireplace. Illuminate it with a flickering light bulb concealed behind the fender. Some careful airbrushing or dry-brush work in the fireplace should accentuate the glow. If you cannot handle brushing try using pastels; they are very effective for weathering.

*L*ogs placed next to the fireplace would be appropriate, and any pine tree provides a convenient source for your supply of small logs. Just pull the needles from a few twigs and use nail clippers to cut the twig into convenient lengths. Stack a few in the log caddy for realistic miniature reproductions of the real thing.

*M*odify an upright piano to make a small pipe organ. Create the pipes from drinking straws cut at an angle and glued together as shown. Cut the slots with the small saw disc in a Dremel Moto Tool or, if you have the patience, with a new blade in a hobby knife. Make the small knobs or stops from cut-off straight pins, pushed in and painted a variety of colors. For a real project, try your hand at one of those massive cathedral pipe organs!

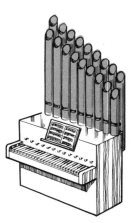

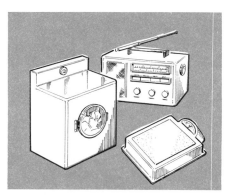

*S*ave those transparent plastic bubbles (or blister) packs from flashlight batteries and similar items. Use your imagination and create clothes washers and dryers, portable radio or record players, terrariums or aquariums.

*N*eed a table lamp? This one is made from a large wooden bead set on a brass ring. Into the top of the bead is glued a piece of drinking straw decorated with a little filigree; the shade is a toothpaste cap over which is glued tiny print material.

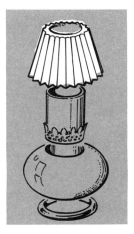

*R*ecognize that lampshade? It began life as a thin plastic coffee creamer container on a restaurant table. Cut out the bottom, trim away the flange (shown dotted), add an insert from an Orville Redenbacher popcorn oil container, glue a tiny bead in the center, and set the whole thing on a miniature wine bottle or a large bead.

*P*lastic 35mm film spools (1-1/2" high) and 120mm spools (about 2-1/2" high) provide the raw materials from which to create lamp bases, sculpture pedestals and more, and they readily accept paint. Both are thrown away by your local film-processing shop, so ask for a few.

*M*ake an oil lamp from a button for the base, two clear glass marbles, a brass necklace fastener, and a short length of clear plastic tube cut from a ballpoint pen refill. Glue it together with a clear-drying glue.

*T*o make frosted glass globes for Victorian gas lights, cut the little stud from Pop-It beads, then remove the pearlized finish with nail polish remover. Glue the bead into a little brass bead cap and attach the completed globe to your chandelier.

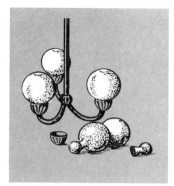

*C*reate beautiful little hanging chandeliers from three-pronged fish hooks and three glass beads. Carefully file or grind off the barbs from the hooks first. Use a good glue to retain the beads on the shanks of the hooks.

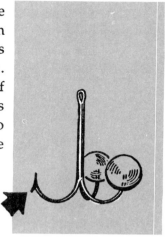

*U*se a clear glass or plastic drawer pull as a very realistic ceiling light. The threaded hole is perfect for accepting a grain-of-wheat bulb. Glue the whole assembly to the ceiling.

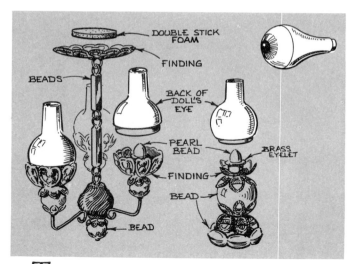

*T*his elegant chandelier and table lamp were very simply assembled from a collection of beads and findings glued together. The lampshades were adapted from the back part of porcelain dolls' eyes, available in many sizes from most craft stores.

*F*or a rich looking candle holder, use the retainer tip from a discarded stick pin. Glued to a suitable base such as a rhinestone or jewelry finding, it can look quite convincing. The rubber insert can be picked out with a pin.

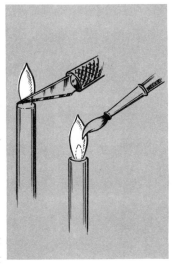

*N*eed mini candles? Find some small cake candles, then sculpt a flame on top with a hobby knife. Dip the "flame" in red nail polish. In reality, candles burn with a yellow flame with a clear cone at the base of the flame. The more artistic candle maker might care to use a yellow translucent lacquer applied with a fine brush. Cut each candle to the correct length when dry.

*H*ere is a simple way to simulate candles in miniature. Cut the cotton bud off Q-Tips cotton swabs — many of which can be found in assorted colors such as pink, yellow, ivory or white, so take your pick. Insert a short length of black thread for a wick and secure it with a drop of white glue. You can even dribble some of that glue down the sides for a little extra realism, too. If you require the candle to be "lit," a sliver of transparent yellow plastic creates a realistic "flame," especially if there is a small light somewhere in the background.

*P*aint various-sized nails and brass wood screws with ivory Liquid Paper correction fluid. Then insert them into suitable beads or brass findings and drip more blobs of Liquid Paper to simulate wax drips. The last operation is to apply a blob of yellow acrylic paint, pulling it upwards to make a flame.

*H*ow about some colored paper Christmas lantern decorations? Fold edges of paper as shown, then again down the center. Snip up as far as the folded edges, then glue the strip to form a tube. Use fine wire or a glued paper strip as a handle and suspend lanterns from a string across your little rooms.

*J*apanese lanterns are always an interesting conversation piece, and they are very easily made. Some fancy toothpicks and cocktail sticks come with a woven paper ball or "pineapple" on the end. Cut this off, glue some beads to it (as shown), then pull through a thread for the hanging. The pineapple variety, when dressed up with some small colored beads and greenery, makes a really attractive seasonal table centerpiece.

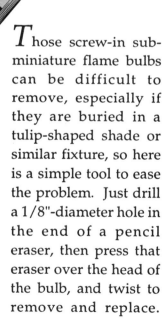

*T*hose screw-in sub-miniature flame bulbs can be difficult to remove, especially if they are buried in a tulip-shaped shade or similar fixture, so here is a simple tool to ease the problem. Just drill a 1/8"-diameter hole in the end of a pencil eraser, then press that eraser over the head of the bulb, and twist to remove and replace.

*H*ere is a suggestion for putting lights inside a china cabinet. You could try using Cir-Kit Concepts #1020-1 clear Christmas tree lights, although similar lights would work. Drill a hole at shelf level and wire the lights together at the back of the cabinet. Glue the lights up under the shelf with the wires led

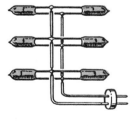

through a hole. Be sure to insulate each wire with a small plastic sleeve, because a short circuit will occur if the wires touch one another. The other diagram shows how the lights can be joined in parallel and connected to a plug. Always follow the manufacturer's instructions.

Need to fill that mini bookcase? Take any magazine having a squared and glued spine, or an inexpensive glued scratch pad, and cut yourself some mini books as shown. Use a new blade and a steel straight edge. Add thin card covers and use those tiny printed illustrations from book club ads to simulate the cover. You can also peel thin leatherette from old diaries.

Do you have an incomplete chess set lying around the house, perhaps a discarded toy? With judicious cutting and gluing, convert them into a rose bowl and a set of book ends. Their usefulness appears limited only by your imagination.

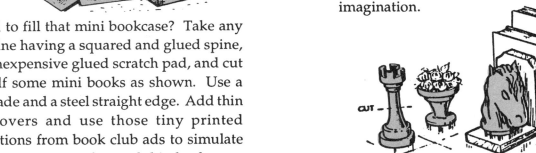

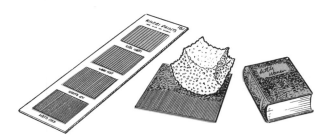

Color chip paint samples from the paint store can be converted to wonderful, leather-look book covers. Spread a drop of matte Mod Podge on the paint sample, stipple it with a sponge, and allow to dry.

Make convincing miniature video tapes. CBS Records Inc. Movie Club provides discount stamps in its advertisements. Clip these stamps and glue them to 1/2" x 7/8" x 3/32"-thick wood or plastic blocks which have been smoothly painted black. If you want to use plastic, ask your local hobby shop for Plastruct sheets which are available in a wide variety of shapes and thicknesses. Glue title blocks to spines and you will have a nice little collection of mini videos for your mini VCR.

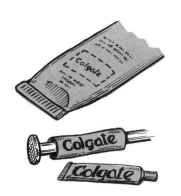

*F*rom the back of an empty Colgate toothpaste tube, cut the little word "Colgate," leaving a good margin of material all round. Roll the piece of toothpaste tube around a nail to make a miniature tube for the bathroom. Crimp one end with pliers, glue a bead into the other, and add a red bead for a cap.

*M*iniature nails are easy to come by, but in many cases the brass or brass-plated ones look wrong on a crate or a fence. Painting them silver doesn't work either. So here's a solution: just cut the heads off some straight pins. However, be sure they are the soft variety — the sort that can be bent easily in your fingers, or you will never be able to cut them with regular wire-cutting pliers. Two types of nails are illustrated: the common or box nail (a), and the horseshoe or cut nail (b). To make the second kind, file off the sides of the head, and it will look like a cut nail when driven home. Note: Don't try to drive these nails into your piece. It's better to assemble it with glue, then drill tiny holes, and press the nails in for effect.

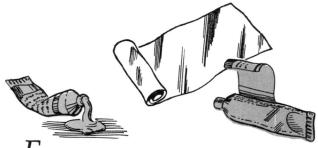

*F*or your miniature artist's studio, here is an effective method of simulating squeezed-out paint tubes. Cut aluminum foil into strips, then roll those strips into cylinders, squeezing the "top" into a cone before gluing on a little tubular bead for the nozzle. Flatten the bottom end with a pair of pliers, adding a few crimps with the point of a knife. Cut the label from glossy magazine paper, and wrap and glue one around each tube. The final touch is to apply that squeezed-out look and a realistic dribble of paint on your artist's table.

*F*or your tiny powder room, here's a simple way to create miniature bars of bath soap. Cut small blocks from your favorite brand of bar soap. Using a hobby knife and a pin, sculpt little bars of soap from the rough blocks, scribing the appropriate design on the top with a pin. (If you take a moment to glue a needle into the end of a short dowel, it makes a useful scriber that will be handy in other projects, too.) Let the bars sit in warm water for a few seconds, and then carefully smooth the rough edges off the etched designs. These designer bars look perfect sitting in a basket on the vanity or on the edge of the bathtub.

If you need to simulate tiny spools of thread, take the dowel from a Q-Tips cotton swab and mark it into 1/8" lengths. Use a little Swiss file to reduce the diameter between the pencil marks, as shown. Paint each spool a different color, then saw them apart with a fine modeler's saw, cleaning up the cut end with fine sandpaper such as No. 600 grit. To complete the illusion, pierce a little hole at each end of the bobbin or spool.

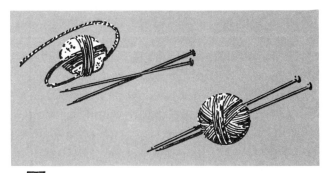

*T*hat mini rocking chair needs some knitting to complete the picture. Take a piece of card or a ball of scrap foam around which you can wrap embroidery thread to form a ball of knitting yarn. Paint a couple of straight pins the color of your choice, then stick them through the ball. You know...you *could* even add a short knitted piece to one of the needles for realism.

*E*very miniature knitting basket must have a supply of yarn. Here's how to make them. Wrap yarn around your fingers until the desired size of skein is achieved. Prepare a small paper label sized to fit, then wrap and glue this label around the skein.

*E*asily create realistic dressmaker's pins for your mini pin cushion. Cut No. 30 jeweler's wire, preferably silver, into 1/2" lengths, then dip the ends in glue. Push the glued end into the cushion; apply various blobs of acrylic paint colors to the protruding end.

*M*ake these attractive pillows using size No. 45 "cover-your-own" buttons. The button loop does not need to be removed — it makes a convenient handle while working on the pillow, and afterwards it usually fits conveniently in the corner of the couch, etc. Notice how lace or ruffle is carefully glued under the edge of each pillow.

*S*ave your perfumed drawer sachets. Remove the contents and refill with cotton to create mini throw cushions. You can also sew them together to make bed covers and tablecloths.

*E*very house needs a calendar, and such miniatures are as close as your wallet. Carefully cut out each month from a little wallet calendar or check register; pierce holes at the top of each page, then thread them on a piece of yarn before hanging them on a wall. Find some tiny pictures from a Book-of-the-Month Club catalogue, and glue them to the top of each page to create a pictorial calendar.

*V*ery attractive fringe can be made by cutting one edge from a suitable length of grosgrain ribbon, then gently unraveling *all the way* to the opposite edge for maximum flexibility. This looks great on rugs, hooded wicker chairs, and more.

*M*iniature sculpting requires miniature sculpting tools — items which are not readily available. You can make your own tools from Fimo, although other sculpting compounds would work equally well. Follow the package directions regarding hardening.

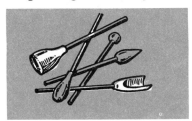

*N*o bathroom or bedroom is complete without the inevitable box of tissues, so here is a way of creating some for your mini rooms. From thin card, cut and fold a box as shown. If you have difficulty folding a neat "square" box, then fold it around a small balsa block sized to the inside dimensions. Before gluing the box, decorate it to resemble your favorite brand, then cut some small squares of tissue to place inside. After the box is glued, your last move is to gently tug at a tissue to leave it peeping properly out of the slot.

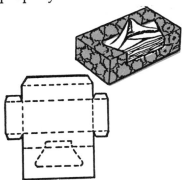

*S*etting up a well-equipped workshop in your dollhouse? Don't spend hours drilling hundreds of holes to make miniature pegboard — get perforated board in various sizes from Radio Shack. (It is normally used for assembling electronic circuits.) Bend your own hook from 24-gauge florist wire. The pegboard looks very nice when framed and carries a good assortment of miniature tools.

*P*erforated paper in a variety of sizes is normally used for cross-stitch; but in the miniatures world it might have been created for dollhouse-size pegboard. Framed with a narrow beading, it looks its best when backed with black paper. Use it to hang tools in your mini workshop or for those hard-to-store kitchen utensils.

*S*tick 8mm-diameter silver-colored beads on toothpicks, then paint with stained glass paints. When dry, glue a silver seed bead over the hole together with a fine wire loop, and you have now created a delightful set of "glass" Christmas tree ornaments.

*M*ake beautiful vases from the 1-1/2"-tall glass contact lens vials your local optician uses. Clean them with alcohol, then paint with a thick poster paint adding any suitable design to taste. You can even add a little fine sand to your paint for interesting textured effects, or glue on mini flowers or beads for a relief design. Finally, drop a lump of clay in the bottom. This

will support the stems of your dried flowers. A thought...these vials would look good in the kitchen, labeled and filled with mini spices or candies.

*D*iscarded Christmas tree lights yield miniature wine or cologne bottles. Close to the base, cut off the two wires, then sand the bottom flat. Glue on a small bead for the stopper and make a suitable label, or look for one in your junk mail that might be small enough to clip out.

*M*any envelopes, when turned inside out, are printed with attractive miniature designs suitable for miniature gift wrapping paper. Add a tiny bow or rosette, and your little parcels are complete.

30

Game boxes — like Monopoly, Pictionary, or Scrabble — are very easily simulated by cutting their pictures from toy catalogs, then gluing the pictures to the appropriate size blocks of wood. Then cover the sides of the blocks with a thin strip of card glued around the edges. These look great when left on your mini coffee table or in the dollhouse young-ster's room.

Look at some of the ads in your junk mail to locate mini credit cards in their correct colors. Carefully clip them from the ad, then coat them with clear nail polish for that stiff, glossy look.

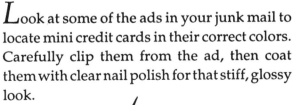

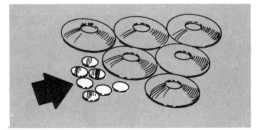

Have you ever noticed those tiny punchings that fall from the center of sequins? Collect a few, paint them silver, and place a mini hand-ful of this "loose change" alongside that purse on the hall table or dresser.

Before junking those out-of-date credit cards, carefully slice off the raised letters and digits. Don't worry if the color has worn off — they can be restored with some careful dry-brushing. They are ideal for miniature signage such as cafeteria menus or profes-sional shingles.

*H*ere is the perfect dollhouse teddy bear, made from pussy willows. Use a colorless, fast sticking glue such as balsa cement to attach various sizes of pussy willows together. Dab in the features with a fine felt tip pen and use a larger marker to apply the black Panda markings if required.

*M*iniature wheels are hard to find and even harder to make. Here's a novel idea: use black dress snaps! They come in different sizes, so a wide selection is available for a variety of projects. The head of the snap can be filed off if it is too tall, then this will allow insertion of a pin or brad as an axle. However, Dritz No. 1/0 snaps are already pierced.

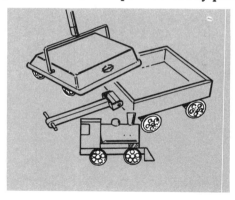

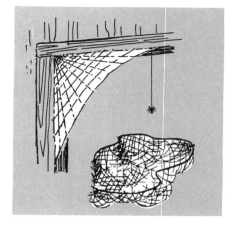

*H*ere is a tip which will be useful around Halloween...cobwebs! From a very fine gray hairnet, cut a piece to fit any convenient corner and secure with dabs of a clear glue, or even rubber cement if you need only a temporary fix. Stretch the net to fit until the desired effect is achieved, then add your own mini, malevolent looking, glittering spider and a-hauntin' we will go. To draw this, your columnist held the pen at arm's length. He hates spiders!

A clear plastic straw, a clear sequin, and a couple of round toothpicks, all assembled as shown here, create a very neat miniature bird feeder. The dowels or perches are made by cutting off the pointed ends of the toothpicks and inserting them through drilled holes in the sides of the straw. (If you do not have small drill bits, it is surprising how effective a hot needle can be when heated over a candle flame.) The *pièce de résistance* is to fill the feeder with coarsely ground pepper, which neatly simulates sunflower seeds.

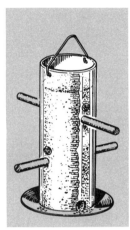

*P*ick up a short off-cut piece of wood molding from your local lumberyard. When sliced as shown, you will have ready-made shelf or porch roof brackets — a foot of material will supply more brackets than you will need in a lifetime! Do any staining before gluing brackets to shelves.

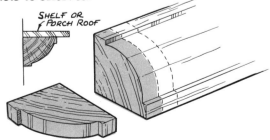

SHELF OR PORCH ROOF

*C*raft an old fashioned ink well and quill pen to decorate your mini desk. Make the ink well from various beads and paint it black. Construct the pen from a feather pulled from a pillow; trim it at the nib end and paint black at the tip.

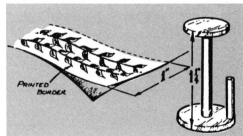

PRINTED BORDER

*A*dd a miniature paper towel roll and holder to your dollhouse kitchen. The holder is made from scraps of basswood and pieces of 1/8" and 1/16" dowel, cut to the height shown. Make the towel roll by peeling off one layer of two-ply paper towel. Cut off a suitable length and trim the width as shown. The card tube is made by loosely winding masking tape, sticky side out, around the center dowel before wrapping the mini paper towel around it.

*S*earch for buttons with interesting or un-usual borders which could be used as picture frames. The rope design around the edge of this one was gilded to produce a very striking highlight to the picture, which was glued into the button. Glaze the picture with several coats of clear nail polish, or even cut a small piece of clear plastic to fit over the picture.

*K*eep an eye open for sweepstakes envelopes and advertising literature for art sales, interior decoration offers, and the like. These frequently carry beautiful miniature reproductions of old masters' paintings. Mount on thin card and coat with a clear urethane varnish. Framed appropriately, these would grace the space above any miniature Victorian fireplace.

*D*on't throw away the clasp from that old multi-strand bead neck-lace! Mount a suitable portrait on thin card, trim it to fit behind the clasp, and attach it with suitable glue to make a perfect gilded framed picture. The little wire fastener at the bottom of the clasp can usually be disguised with a small bow or suitable beads.

*H*ere's a clever way to simulate a gilded picture frame. First, make a wooden frame in the usual way, then cut strips from a full-size doily, gluing them to the face of the wooden frame as shown. Be sparing with the glue so that you do not fill in the detail. When the glue has dried, spray with gold paint.

*M*ake inexpensive art by cutting min-iature pictures from *Architectural Digest* magazine. Glue them to a thin card, apply clear varnish, then glue thin foam directly to the picture after staining or gilding the pieces. We recommend cutting the picture just a little smaller than the framing so that card edges are not visible.

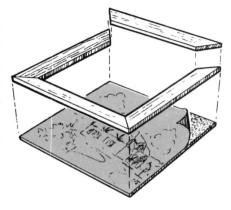

*A*re you looking for a way to simulate a modern metal picture frame? Try metallic pressure sensitive tapes from graphics supply stores and Chartpak or Letraset brands, which are commonly available. Cut your pieces of wood framing to size, then wrap each piece with a strip of the tape which can be embossed with a blunt scriber to produce ribbing or whatever other design you desire. Your columnist also suggests that if you know a local model plane enthusiast, you might ask him if he has any remnants of metallic Monokote heat-activated covering material. This will do a good job of covering and shrinking onto your wood pieces.

*I*t is very simple to make attractive simulated wicker picture or mirror frames. First make a frame of balsa wood, then wrap the frame with waxed linen cord using one or more colors of your choice. When complete, the picture or mirror can then be glued to the back of the frame. Little flowers glued into each corner make a highly attractive furnishing.

*F*rame botanicals to look as though they are covered with glass. Craft and stationery stores stock transparent laminating plastic — all you do is peel back the top layer, set the botanicals in place, and then press the top layer firmly back into place. Trim around with a pair of shears, then make yourself a frame from the wood of your choice, stained and varnished.

*H*ere's an easy way to hang pictures. Rubber cement strips of magnetic material, 3/8"-wide and a little narrower than the picture, to the dollhouse wall. Cement a larger piece to the back of the picture — the final result gives you some flexibility in the positioning of your pictures. Before gluing the magnets to the picture, try twisting them around to check the orientation that gives the greatest attraction. Magnetic strips can be found in some of the more exotic business cards, refrigerator appliques, and at Radio Shack.

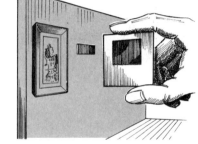

*S*ave that saw-edged strip of metal from your box of kitchen foil or plastic wrap. By cutting strips from it, using metal shears or heavy scissors, then molding suitable handles from Fimo, you can create any type of saw you wish — from a kitchen bread knife to a cross-cut saw for the woodshed. Just bake the Fimo right onto the metal, using tan or brown colors as required.

*T*his grate will look nice in any kitchen. All you need is a paper clip and a small piece of aluminum from a soft drink can. Mark and punch the aluminum using a small sharp nail. Cut the paper clip to leave a U shape, then fold the aluminum around the legs of the U. Be sure to have the rough side outermost.

*T*his incredible little steak knife is just about 1" long. Use shears to cut a narrow strip of metal from the cutting edge of a box of foil, then carve the tiny handle from a piece of basswood. Stain it and add rivets with dots from a fine point marker pen. Secure the blade into the handle with a tiny drop of strong glue.

*S*ome kitchens I have seen have neatly framed pegboards from which hang the best pots, pans and utensils. A useful source of miniature pegboards is the notions counter which usually offers perforated cross-stitch paper — just right for 1" scale. When framed with basswood and appropriately painted, it looks good on your kitchen wall. Make little hooks from bright paper clip wire or staples. Stiff paper can also be used to create free-standing fire screens, trellis arches, and more.

*S*tock that kitchen cupboard with boxes of macaroni, cereal, Jello, and more. How? Search out those brightly colored discount coupons. Clip out the picture of the product and glue them on to suitably sized blocks of wood after covering them with plain paper. If you are not too concerned about exact scale, then the sky's the limit for a well-stocked pantry.

*C*anned goods, cookie boxes, candy bars... all in miniature. Discount coupons frequently provide little reproductions of brand name labels. Paint lengths of dowel silver for the cans; glue the miniature labels to strips of thin glossy paper and wrap them around the cans. Cookie or cracker boxes start life as blocks of wood, which are then wrapped and labeled. And a bar of Fimo, wrapped in foil with label applied, makes a mouthwatering candy bar. Your columnist gained five pounds just typing this...!

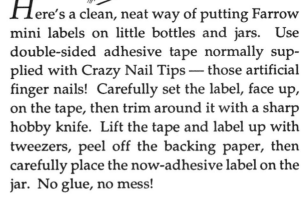

*H*ere's a clean, neat way of putting Farrow mini labels on little bottles and jars. Use double-sided adhesive tape normally supplied with Crazy Nail Tips — those artificial finger nails! Carefully set the label, face up, on the tape, then trim around it with a sharp hobby knife. Lift the tape and label up with tweezers, peel off the backing paper, then carefully place the now-adhesive label on the jar. No glue, no mess!

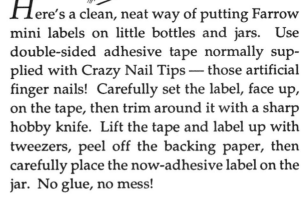

*M*ake this crystal candy dish by merely cutting the knob off the back of a suction cup, then gluing the plastic cup to a suitable button. Fill with tiny cake decorator's sprinkles, then cover with a second plastic suction cup to which a wooden handle or knob has been glued. These clear plastic suction cups can also double as crystal cereal bowls, too.

*T*o form pots and jugs out of Sculpey or Fimo, spray the end of a suitable size dowel with a cooking shortening — the finished article slides off easily and is ready for firing. Trim all edges while the piece is still on the dowel.

*C*ollect the casings and tops from Avon brand lipstick samples. Cut them down, add wire or card strip handles coated heavily with polyurethane enamel, and you have created miniature beer steins. If you are artistically inclined, paint miniature scenes on the sides.

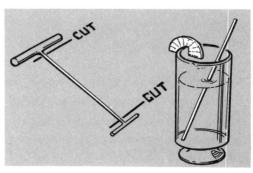

*W*ine and champagne glasses can be constructed from a sequin base, wire or bead stem, and the clear end of a medicine capsule case. Just go easy on the glue for a neat job.

*L*ooking around for a source of straws for tall mini drinks? Plastic ties that secure labels and price tags to clothing work perfectly. Simply cut them as shown in the illustration.

*S*words into plowshares! Would you believe that these miniature ice cream soda glasses started out as ammunition? Your local toy store probably carries these soft vinyl Flex-I-Tip "bullets" for the Hawk air pump guns. Add a 7mm pompon, dress it up with a red seed bead, cut a nylon bristle from a brush for the straw, and you'll have a mini ice cream soda.

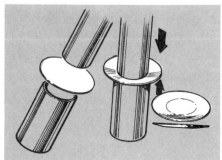

*A*fter cutting appropriately sized discs from stiff paper, use the two parts of a lipstick container as a die press to give mini picnic plates their shape. Simply center the disc on the cover, then gently press the other half into (but not through) the paper disc.

*L*ook in the fingernail polish section of your drugstore for tiny acrylic nail decals. They are inexpensive — about $1 for twenty on a sheet, and they depict birds, flowers, nondescript designs, etc. When used on mini plates and chinaware, they completely transform the look. Appropriate designs can also be used on furniture, particularly in children's rooms of the dollhouse.

*H*ere's a neat source of cereal bowls for your miniature kitchen cabinet. Carefully slice out the little plastic pallets from a model paints package to create a respectable stack of bowls.

*P*lastic bubble packs around some merchandise (and perhaps even L'Eggs containers) can be altered to make a neat barbecue grill. Trim to the required size. Cut three dowels,

paint silver with black "feet," then glue into holes in the plastic. Add the dished ash catcher. Make handles from ordinary office staples. Glue a piece of wood to the top, and then paint the grill a nice, shiny black.

*T*he pump tops from hand lotion and liquid soap bottles make fine spigots for your mini sink. Look for chrome and gold pumps — they are available.

*O*ld earrings can be converted into soup spoons and ladles with very little effort. Just remove the decorative part, pick out the glue, then paint the item silver or copper. They also make very nice drawer pulls, too.

*S*pilled liquid is readily simulated with melted hot glue. Lightly painted with acrylic colors, it can be made to resemble coffee, milk, lemonade, etc.

*T*hese delicious looking doughnuts are nothing more than Cheerios cereal touched up with a little acrylic paint, then sprayed with a clear lacquer or clear nail varnish. Glue them on a plate or make a little doughnut box.

*C*reate beautifully realistic ham and eggs in miniature. The eggs are made by dropping a small amount of white porcelain touchup on a plate. The yoke is the center bead from artificial flowers — the bead being cut in half and pressed

into the enamel as it dries. The ham is clipped from a color super market meat counter advertisement, then glued to a thin piece of balsa wood, the edge of the wood being colored with the appropriate pink marker pen. Finally, the whole meal is set on a high class white plate which was extracted from the cap of a quart size soda bottle.

*T*his is a completely new use for wide, flat rubber bands! Cut and trimmed, then decorated with red marker pens and white paint, they make convincing bacon slices. M-m-m! Can almost smell it crisping in that mini fry pan. Check the appearance with a real slice from your refrigerator.

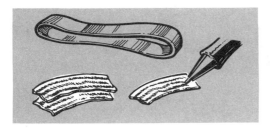

*T*hese delicious looking miniature steaks actually are edible — if you happen to be a dog! Look for dog food nuggets from Tender Chops by Ken-L Ration. Place them in your dollhouse broiler or on the grill. For a glossy look, just coat them with clear glaze or fingernail polish.

Cut a small wedge-shaped piece from the cork found inside of a bottle cap. Then, perhaps, use a little acrylic paint to color the cork as desired. What do we have? A pie of course, with one piece removed! Try adding a thin layer of white spackle to simulate cream topping or meringue.

Miniature cake and gift boxes are difficult to fold and achieve that convincing crisp look. To aid the process, cut an appropriately sized wood block around which all folding should be done. Remove the block once all gluing is completed.

Depending on how they are painted, cork stoppers can become whatever you wish — a cake, a pie or a cheese! Cake icing can be represented by heavily applied swirls of acrylic paint, or perhaps even spackle. And the perforated texture of cork makes a great blue cheese.

*N*eed mini cotton candy for your soda shop? Roll a little paper tube (or use a piece cut from a cotton swab), and decorate it with a red marker pen. Then glue a fluffed-up cotton ball around it. The cotton can be colored with a pink marker or sprayed with pink artist color, such as Dri-Mark, from your art supply store.

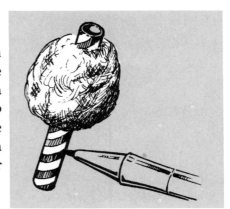

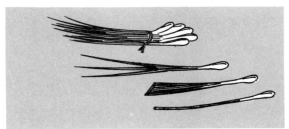

*F*ashion very convincing miniature spring onions from a packet of white stamens from the craft store. Wet the ends and flatten with your thumbnail before cutting slits to form the leaves.

*E*ver wondered where to obtain miniature popcorn? Crumble pieces of expanded plastic foam — such as Styrofoam. String pieces onto fine sewing thread to create miniature garlands. This popcorn would look good in front of your mini television set, too, with a can of the appropriate beverage! Your columnist suggests you might give the foam beads the merest dusting of yellow paint from an airbrush, for an even more authentic "buttered" look.

*M*ake convincing miniature roses. First, run a red marker along the very edge of a narrow, pink ribbon; roll to form the rose. The end result is a rose with petals tinted a natural looking red. Add a green stem and a leaf or two for the final touch.

*C*reate miniature ferns simply and inexpensively. The next time you pick up your dry cleaning, save the twist-ties which are usually larger than your average garbage bag variety. Cut them to the shape shown, then with the end of a pair of sharp pointed scissors, make a series of cuts up each side. The complete fern leaves can then be curved to shape, then "planted" in a mini pot of clay. If the shade of green is not quite right for your purpose, paint the tie with acrylic paint before cutting the fronds.

*T*o make mini trees, find suitable weeds with tiny leaves. Dry and spray paint to suit. To increase the density of the foliage, cut additional sprigs at an angle, then hot glue them to the sides of the main "trunk."

*S*mall pine cones can be made into realistic cactuses. Remove the top section from the cone. Paint the remaining cone with olive green acrylic, then pot when dry. Glue a crown of tiny straw flowers to the top if you wish it to appear in bloom.

CUT

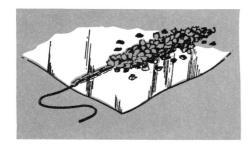

*E*asily create realistic vines. Cut a piece of fine string the length required, plus 3". Coat all except the end 3" with white glue and lay it on a piece of waxed paper. Now, sprinkle parsley flakes on the string, patting them firmly into the glue before turning the string over and repeating the process. Pick up the string and tie the free end to a coat hanger, allowing it to dry before winding the vine around a trellis.

*T*iny real flowers suitable for drying are not always available in naturally occurring colors. Find a variety of very small white flowers, then place the stems in small vials of food coloring diluted with water. The petals will soon turn the color of the dye. The flowers may then be dried using a commercial drying gel.

*H*ere is a novel use for pipe cleaners — flowers! Clip about 3/8" from a pipe cleaner, then fold it in two around a short length of floral wire. Use a dab of clear glue to attach the pipe cleaner to the wire. Next, attach a few leaves clipped from floral paper. If you have not been able to obtain colored pipe cleaners, you can now dye the bloom with food coloring.

*N*eed some mini cattails in a hurry? Put glue on the end of a piece of florist's wire, then dip it into powdered instant coffee. Stick the wire into clay or Styrofoam until dry.

Many everyday products can form the basis of furnishings for miniature rooms. Here are some examples: The jar started life as a bottle of roll-on office glue. Plaster over, add Sculpey handles and paint to make an Indian vase. The planter was the cap from a bottle. The kitchen garbage can started life as the cap from a marking pen. Make the lid from painted card.

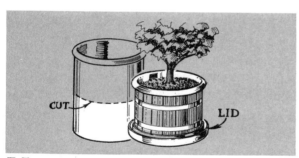

Very inexpensive planters can be made from discarded black plastic 35mm film containers. Just cut the container where you desire and press the cap onto the cut edge, the cap now forming the water trough around the base. If black does not suit your scheme, then scribe "planks" on the planter, wipe with alcohol, then paint with suitable acrylic color. Add bands of self-adhesive brass foil as trim. Fill planters with desired foliage.

Make this attractive fern or plant stand. Twist three pieces of wire together tightly. Then form the feet as shown. Carefully measure the holder at the top against your miniature plant pot, then form the supports as shown. If you use bright plated brass wire, you only need apply clear nail lacquer to retain the bright finish. An alternate method is to apply a matte black paint for a wrought iron look.

Need a seaweed for your mini collector's box or aquarium? Crack an almond nut or two and carefully extract the fibrous "packing" from around the kernel — it makes perfect miniature seaweed. Why not dye it to suit your purpose using vegetable dyes?

*I*f you are looking for miniature bark mulch for your dollhouse garden, then try loose tea liberally sprinkled among the plants. It looks extremely realistic, and the aroma is also yours to choose — jasmine, Darjeeling, orange pekoe.

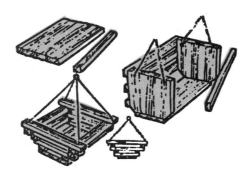

*C*onvert leftover cedar shingles into planters for miniature greenhouses. Score some of the shingles along the grain to make strips 1/8" wide. Trim other shingles to make ends or bases, then glue together as shown in the sketches. For the hangers, use fine floral wire, old jewelry chain, or chain from the model railroad store. The rough finish to the wood strips offers a very authentic look to the items.

*N*eed a hanging planter? Take appropriately shaped ballpoint pen caps and cut to length. Trim out the lip to make them appear thinner, then fill the pots with your favorite mini kitchen plants. Prepare a piece of wood with holes, set the pots in place, and suspend the whole assembly from four cords or discarded jewelry chain. Chain can also be obtained from hobby stores selling model ship or train fittings.

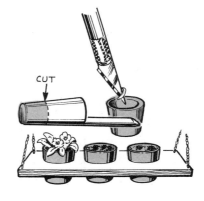

CUT

*H*aving a little difficulty getting that lady doll to remain standing? Here is one solution: pierce the bottom of a paper Dixie cup, turn it upside down, then force the lady's legs through the slits until her feet touch the ground. She can now stand without difficulty and her long skirts will effectively conceal the paper cup.

*T*hose half-dolls used for cake decorating are ideal for mini projects, except that they have no legs. Here's how to make some useful 5-1/4"-tall dolls from them. With a hot ice pick or large nail, pierce a hole in the end of one half of a L'Eggs pantyhose container. Insert the point of the doll into the hole and secure with a suitable glue. When set, the doll will stand with floor length dresses flaring nicely to cover container.

*D*id you know that an inexpensive gold necklace could quickly become a mini pocket watch? Use the clasp for the watch case (removing the little clasp knob), and punch a face from a piece of slick paper. Use a fine crow quill pen — or a 4 x 0 drafting pen — to make the Roman numerals and hands, then glue the face onto the clasp. I would advise putting the face into the clasp, *then* applying glue at the back. One could even punch a clear plastic disc for the watch glass. A short piece of gold wire on one end and a suitable bead for the fob on the other complete the illusion.

*H*ere's how to make mini reading glasses. Tape together three toothpicks, with the center one cut short. Wind on the fine wire as shown, pulling it tight and securing the crossover with a tiny drop of glue, then bending the side pieces after you've slid them off the toothpicks. To make lenses, you can either cut little acetate discs which are then glued in place, or lay the frames on wax paper and drop in a blob of white glue which dries clear. You can also go to a store specializing in plastic model plane kits and pick up a tube of Krystal Kleer which is made for that purpose.

*B*eautiful miniature hats can be made from small lace medallions or from little lace doilies. Merely dip the lace into Hazel's Doily Dip, or a similar draping product, and drape and mold the lace over a suitable form such as a gum ball machine plastic container or a Saran-wrapped wood form. Remove when dry and trim lace with miniature flowers.

*T*o produce true-to-scale buttons on mini garments, use a toothpick to apply drops of porcelain repair paint (from the hardware store). The more coats applied, the larger the button becomes. Your columnist offers this — leave the paint to develop a firm skin, then use a flattened toothpick to squash the droplet to true button shape. Now use a fine brush and perhaps a magnifier to paint on the holes and stitches.

*H*ere's a trick borrowed from an HO railroad modeler: when painting, set your pieces on a slightly moist sponge. The rough surface of the sponge holds the items securely, in spite of the sponge being tilted to seemingly impossible angles.

*T*o apply stain or paint in hard-to-reach places such as between stair rail spindles, use those little padded foam eye shadow applicators. These are inexpensively obtained from the make-up department of your local dime store.

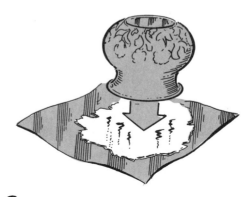

*S*ometimes the rim of a ceramic pot or jar requires a carefully painted thin edging, and that can be tricky to accomplish in such a small scale. Apply a thin coat of paint to a piece of waxed paper, then carefully press the rim of the jar into the still wet paint, giving it a little twist as you do to ensure an even coating to the rim.

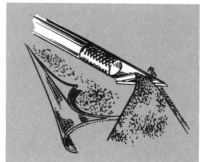

*D*o you need ultra-thin fake leather to cover that mini chair? A remnant of vinyl upholstery material or a piece from an old purse can often be split apart from its fabric backing using a sharp blade, then carefully peeled apart to leave the thinnest upholstery material you have ever seen. Great for covering books, too!

*I*f your dollhouse has any small, hard-to-get-at rooms which are difficult to decorate, assemble the room as a separate box and then set it in place when it's complete. It is much easier to work on the room at your workbench. This bathroom is a good example.

*I*f you transport your dollhouses to many shows, here's a method of safely moving your room boxes. Invest in some cat litter boxes. Fold a towel into each litter box, then place each room box on this. Apart from acting as a cushion under the box while traveling, it also doubles as a lift-out device when you grasp the ends of the towel. You might also be able to pick up some inexpensive plastic or fiberboard tote boxes for the same purpose.

*P*ins have a tendency to leave large unsightly holes in delicate pieces. When pinning temporarily while the glue dries, use small sewing needles and use pointed pliers to insert them. They enter the wood easily and the hole can hardly be seen after withdrawal. Usually a spot of water will swell the wood enough to eliminate the hole without resorting to filler putty.

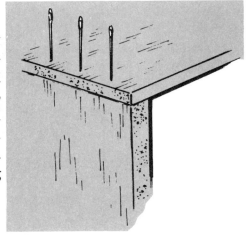

*C*ertain decorating ideas require a pencil line around each room's walls, equidistant from the floor all the way around. The answer? Tape a pencil to a wooden block, then adjust the height of the block until the pencil draws the line at the required height.

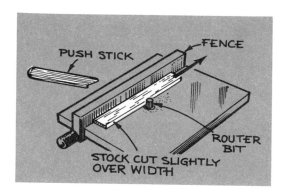

*I*f you need a series of strips, all identical width, there is a far easier and more reliable method of achieving your goal if you have access to a small router table. Cut strips by hand and very slightly over-width. Set the router fence the desired distance from the edge of the router bit, then run a couple of test strips through to check the finished dimension. If this is satisfactory, run the remainder. We used a 1/4" straight bit set slightly higher than the thickness of the stock, and found that this method is more reliable and cuts cleaner than a table saw. You need one good finished edge to run against the guide fence to start with. Be sure to use a push stick to move strips through the router to save your fingers!

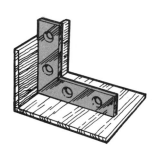

*W*hen gluing parts at 90° angles to each other, the regular students' triangles are cumbersome to use on miniatures. Your hardware store probably yields a nice line of metal corner brackets, ranging in size from 1" to 3" — just right for our hobby use.

*H*ave you ever considered using Velcro to attach removable fronts or roofs? Use a piece on each corner. Your columnist also suggests using a small piece of tinplate (not aluminum) in each corner and a short piece of strip magnet (from Radio Shack) for the same purpose.

*T*racing a pattern onto dark wood or leather leaves an image difficult to discern — here's a simple solution. Cut around the pattern, lay it on the wood (perhaps with a smear of rubber cement to hold it), then spray over with an aerosol powder such as Dr. Scholl's Foot Powder. Peel off the pattern and you will be left with a perfectly defined outline.

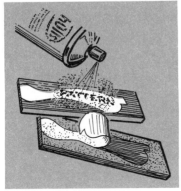

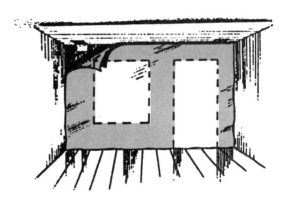

*I*t can be very difficult to obtain the exact shape of a piece of wallpaper to go into an assembled dollhouse. This trick makes it a little easier. Tape a piece of carbon paper into the house with carbon side facing you. Lay thin notepaper over that, then burnish with your thumbnail or a spatula. Pay particular attention to edges of door openings, etc. Remove notepaper, then cut along carboned lines to generate the template for your wallpaper piece. We suggest gluing in door and window trims *after* room is papered.

*K*eep a card file system for your ideas — it makes future information retrieval so much easier when you are in need of that "bright idea" for your project. For example, when reading through *Nutshell News* magazine, make a note of items on a card for future reference: "Christmas Rooms, NN 12/81, pg. 8."

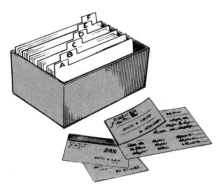

*I*f you are in the habit of attending shows and gathering business cards and literature, then you will need to develop some form of information retrieval system. One such system is an indexed 3-1/2" x 5" file card system. Staple the business card to a file card, then list all that manufacturer's offerings on the same file card. It is also very useful to develop a second card system which indexes by products and cross references to the first system. For example, list everything by products — Wiring systems, Finishes, Miniature paintings, etc.

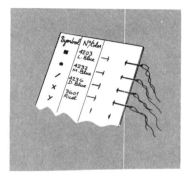

*K*eep your needlepoint organized. Prepare a 3" x 5" card, listing all your colors and symbols as shown. Pierce small holes along the edge of the card and into these holes insert the threaded needles, returning the needles to the holes after each use. This keeps your colors organized and free of tangles.

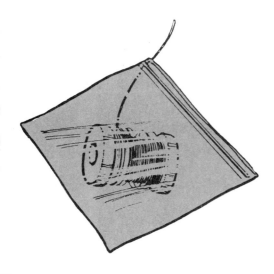

*I*f you happen to be running out of room on your workbench, you might find these little storage containers a great space saver. They are fishing tackle containers found in a sporting goods store and are stacked by screwing one into the other. The price is the great part — under $1!

*S*pools of fine wire have a nasty habit of springing unwound from the bobbin. This can be prevented by imprisoning the bobbin in a close fitting Zip-Loc poly bag and feeding the end of the wire out through the corner.

*G*lue tubes have a nasty habit of dripping on your work area between uses. Stand them up in paper cups to eliminate this problem. Shown here are several paper cups glued to a board for greater stability.

*T*his is a really clever way to retrieve those tiny items which fall and became lost in the pile of your rug. Cut a piece from a pair of discarded pantyhose, then rubber band it over the vacuum cleaner pipe. Vacuum the area where the part fell and you will no doubt find it firmly held by the nylon screen.

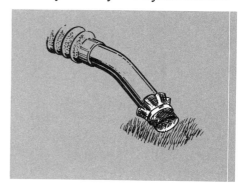

*T*he problem with a hot glue gun is that one never quite knows where to park it after use. Convert a wire cup holder to support your glue gun between applications. If you don't have a cup holder, an old coat hanger is a ready source of easily formed wire from which you can manufacture your own. Note the old spoon attached to catch the drips!

*M*any miniaturists use a glue syringe in their work, but obviously find blockages occurring due to the glue drying out at the end of the needle. Here's a simple cure — stick the end of the needle into a rubber knitting needle protector immediately after each glue application. This seals the glue away from the air.

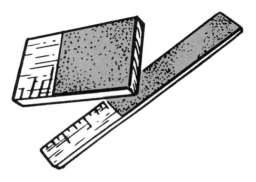

A yardstick cut into 2" sections with a 1-1/2" strip of sandpaper wrapped and glued around each piece makes useful little sanding blocks, especially if you make some with different grades of sandpaper. Your columnist also finds that longer ones with a handle left at one end are equally useful for many jobs.

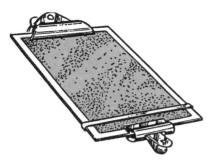

A very useful item to have on your workbench is a sandpaper board on which the grade of sandpaper may be quickly changed. The answer is an inexpensive clipboard, a paper gripper and a rubber band employed as shown here.

*H*ere is one of the handiest sanding blocks I have ever seen. This is a 1" x 8" x 11" marble slab — a remnant from a stone mason's yard — which has three pieces of sandpaper glued on each surface (six in all), each different. The slab is anchored to the bench by its own weight, and the friction of the sandpaper on the underside prevents the slab from sliding around. You have six different grits, from coarse down to fine, and a perfectly flat surface to boot!

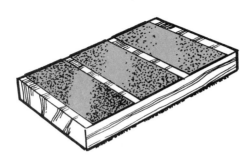

*T*he regular miniature saw table has grooves which tend to prevent easy movement of the piece you are cutting. Cut a slot in a piece of Plexiglas, then attach it to the regular saw table with a strip of masking tape at each corner or with double-stick tape. The close-fitting slot around the blade stops the tiny pieces of wood from disappearing down the hole around the blade and the wood pieces also glide smoothly over the plastic table.

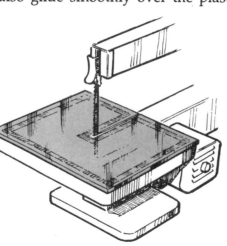

*S*ometimes one is required to drill a blind hole to a certain depth (a blind hole is one that does not go all the way through). But the big question is, "How will I know when to stop?" If one is required to drill a 1/2"-deep hole in a piece of wood, then measure 1/2" up the drill and wind a piece of adhesive tape around it at that point. Now drill into the wood until the tape just touches the surface of the wood. You will have a hole the required depth.

*H*ere is a tip from a friendly shoemaker! If you are using a knife in this manner to pare away at a piece of wood, you stand a very good chance of a divided thumb. Cut the finger from an old leather glove. Punch holes around the lower edge, thread a piece of elastic through it, then slip this finger stall over your threatened thumb for maximum protection from that sharp-edged blade.

*A*nother earring tip: with the decorative piece removed, the remaining ear clamp serves as an ideal clamp when gluing very small pieces.

*T*he silk canvasses for miniature needle-point are very expensive, so why waste money using the regular large hoops? Cut a hole in a piece of stiff card, large enough to accommodate your piece of work, then tape the appropriate size of canvas to the back. We only show two pieces of tape, but four should be used.

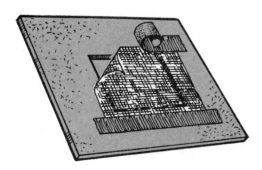

*Y*et another use for those baggie ties — as a source of fine, soft pliable wire in an emergency. Just peel or slice off the paper wrapping and scrape any remainder away with a blunt blade. You now have some useful wire for a variety of jobs. A great idea when you run out of wire on a Sunday evening after the stores are closed!

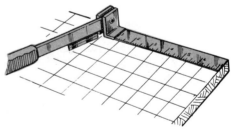

*T*his is a very useful update to a strip wood chopper. Obtain a Stanley steel rule, which is graduated down to 1/64", and glue it to the chopper base, making sure that the 1" graduation is exactly 1" from the cutting edge of the blade. If you can get your rule closer to the cutting edge than I have shown, so much the better. This tool makes it so much easier to do repetitive cuts with consistency — such as when you need ladder rungs all the same length.

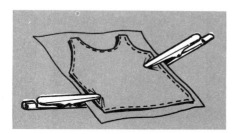

*U*se micro alligator clips (found in Radio Shack) to hold paper patterns in place on material. They can be readily moved around to facilitate cutting.

*I*f you break the pin drills supplied with mini hardware, make your own by grinding the point from a needle, then carefully grind a three-cornered point. *Do use safety glasses when using a grinder.*

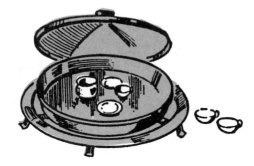

*I*nstead of using an 8000-watt oven to fire your Fimo or Sculpey pieces, try an 8-1/2"-diameter oven from the supermarket. Set the oven on a 2000-watt burner — it does the job equally well... and a lot cheaper!

*I*f you have access to a bandsaw, cut a roll of paper towel into three or four sections — pull off small "towelettes" while you are working. Shown is a simple holder from scrap wood and coat hanger wire which can hang from the edge of your bench. Actually, if you cut off just one section from the roll and return the remainder to the kitchen, perhaps nobody will notice!

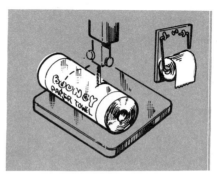

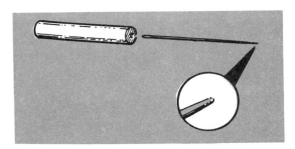

*D*id you know you can make Size 00 knitting needles from darning needles? Obtain a packet of darning needles size 14/18, which are about 3" long. Blunt the end on #600 emery paper or better still on a fine oil stone, leaving the end rounded but polished smooth. Drill small holes in the ends of 3"-long pieces of 3/8" dowel, then glue the needles into it to form handles. Our contributor remarks that she finds an empty Polident container is just perfect for storing these needles.

A useful tool for rushing seats is as close as your supermarket. Cut a bamboo skewer to 3" to 4" lengths. Attach the appropriate length of string and wind it around as shown — the continuous length eliminates the necessity of tying and hiding so many knots.

*M*ake saw cuts halfway through a yardstick. Push T-pins into the ends of items to be stained or painted, and use the T-pin as a handle. After painting, slide the T-pin into the slots, allowing the piece to hang while drying. The yardstick can be supported across the backs of two chairs.

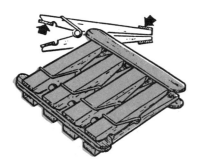

*T*his indispensable spring vise clamp is made by gluing popsicle sticks (arrowed) to spring clothespins. It is useful for many jobs — gluing panels to miniature doors, for instance. The clamp can be used as a "third hand" or held between the knees. It could even be used by gluing it to one end of the workbench.

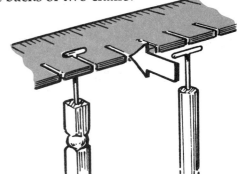

*G*reat idea for those sharp tools! Protect the cutting ends or edges by slipping them into the finger holes of old leather gloves. Your columnist suggests removing the fingers from the gloves, then stapling them to a strip of wood which can be tacked over the back of the workbench. A little oil worked into the leather keeps corrosion off the tools.

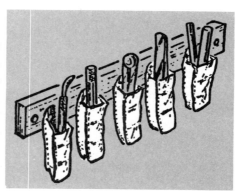

*T*his is a really smart idea borrowed from jewelers. Use thumb tacks to attach an apron to the underside of your workbench edge, then tie the apron around your waist when working. Any small parts dropped or accidentally swept over the edge will be caught by the apron, eliminating the need to grovel among the sawdust and shavings on the floor. Your contributor also warns — obviously from experience — to make sure the telephone and coffee pot are within arm's reach!

A foam drinking cup with a stone wedged inside for added stability makes a useful "pin cushion." An alternative method (shown in diagram), which is often used by model builders, is to cut a foam disc to form a lid for the cup. Fill part of the cup with dry sand, glue and press in the foam lid; when dry, invert the cup.

If you need to cut paper circles, insert an X-Acto swivel stencil cutting knife into an inexpensive school compass. Now you can cut perfect circles of any size.

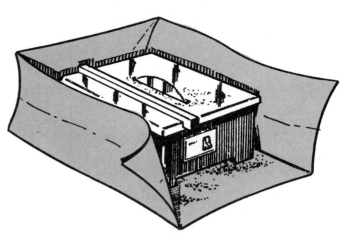

Some fumble thumbs could benefit from this suggestion. To give your hobby knife a little more bulk to grasp, push a short section of rubber hose over the knurled grip part. You could even wrap a thick layer of tape around the handle — although this causes some difficulty when you need to change the blade.

Many a miniaturist's kitchen or living room has to do double duty as a workshop in addition to its regular function. In an effort to keep clean-up to a minimum, contain the dust from your little table saw by opening up a paper grocery bag as shown and standing the saw in that. Although at first glance it might seem to be inconvenient, in actuality it is not as restrictive as you might imagine.

Index